Emmanuel: The Christmas Presence

Meditations on the Symbols of Christmas

Alan Bragwell

DEDICATION

Thanks to God the Father, for sending
His Son, through the power of the Holy
Spirit. For us. To be free. "Thanks be to
God, for His indescribable gift!"
2 Corinthians 9:15

Cover Design by Meagan Gaston
Bragwell

Art Activities by Debra Williams
Bragwell

CONTENTS

Forward   i

1   The Tree   1

2   Colors of the Holiday   Pg 5

3   Décor and the Tree   Pg 7

4   Biblical Emblems   Pg 13

5   Children and Christmas   Pg 16

6   Emmanuel   Pg 18

7   The Advent Wreath   Pg 23

8   God's Gift   Pg 27

9   The Second Advent   Pg 32

10   Neat Family Stuff to Do   Pg 34

11   Photo Explanations   Pg 39

FORWARD

I love Christmas, because I love Jesus. To me, part of the holiday is about getting connected with one another, staying connected, as well as transmitting our stories, and family stories, and most importantly, transmitting His story. A number of years ago, I wanted to provide the congregation where I served some materials that would help them enjoy the Christmas holiday even more. After presenting a Christmas message, I published the outline as an insert in the weekly bulletin for several years. Years later, it was placed it on my website, and also as an annual post on Facebook, which I continued for a number of years. I had not updated since the original release. After recently publishing my first book I have brought forward this book. My intent is not for this to be some sort of "Encyclopedia of Christmas", but simply a companion item to be on the book or coffee table as a quick reference and stimulator of thought and meditation. The first Christmas was a fulfillment of promise. I pray that it is a blessing to the reader, and that it can be a companion to your holiday traditions and activities in your home and family. Emmanuel. God with us.

1 THE TREE

Isaiah 41:17-20; 60:13; 11:1-5; Psalm 1:3;
Matthew 3:10; Galatians 3:13; Revelation
22:2, 14; Exodus 37:1-2.

In the beginning, God created trees. God
loves trees. Through history the tree has
been and continues to be a powerful
symbol of life. History is truly divided
by a tree made into a cross. And at the
end of it all, there will be a tree, as
described in Revelation 22:14. A cut tree
is a reminder of the Cross of the Lord
Jesus Christ. It can also be a strong
reminder of our need to bear fruit.
Christ taught about how a tree would be
pruned in order to bear more fruit. (John
15:2) In heaven is the Tree of Life, as
are other trees in God's presence. When
it is time to place the tree in our homes,
things happen. We start planning,
moving furniture, getting boxes out of

the attic or storage with the ornaments, and begin that process of decoration. In many ways, the tree is an inconvenience in our home. But we make room for the tree, and it is generally given a place of centrality and prominence during the season. The tree reminds us of how we too, must make room for Jesus in our homes and lives, in a central location.

The tradition of decorating a tree in a home is generally credited to Martin Luther, who started the practice in Germany in the mid 15th Century. It was said, "Devout Christians brought decorated trees into their homes." The first decorations were said to be food, cookies, nuts, and eventually, candles as lights (a risky proposition on a dry tree).

Over time, the tradition expanded to the hanging of emblems and symbols of our lives on the tree, as well as symbols of God, and the first Christmas. For many families, one can see the history or major points of emphasis of life, just by looking at their Christmas tree. The Christmas tree can be a tremendous way to transmit the message of Christ to our family, our children, and our neighbors.

Suggested Activity: Be sure to share the stories of each ornament, its meaning and history to your family. It is the stories that last for children.

2 THE DOMINANT COLORS OF THE HOLIDAY

We all are familiar with the basic colors of Christmas, but we may not be aware of the roots and deeper meanings of them, from a Biblical perspective.

The Color Green--Revelation 4:3. Green is the color of life and God's Throne.

The Color Red-- I Corinthians 11:25; Hebrews 9:13-14; I Peter 1:19.
The Blood of Christ, and the color of covenant.

The Color Gold--Revelation 21:18, 21; Matthew 2:11: Exodus 25. Gold is the color of God's presence, riches, and our duty of obedience to Him.

The Color Silver--Malachi 3:3; Psalm 12:6; 66:10. It is the color of redemption and ransom. The sockets in the Tabernacle were silver representing the place where God touches man.

The Color Royal Blue-- Exodus 26: 31-37; Revelation 4:3; I Corinthians 15:47-49. Royal blue is the color of the expectation of the heavenly visit and gift. The veil of the Tabernacle, the entrance to God's presence, was this color.

The Color White-- Matthew 1:21-23. White: the color of purity, sinlessness, and of Christ's Virgin Birth.

3 DÉCOR AND THE TREE

The Circle-- Isaiah 9:6. The eternal nature of God can be represented in a circle. So much can be said of the circle, but its main reflection is of eternity; unending.

Clear Lights-- John 1:9; 8:12; 1 John 1:5. Jesus, the Light of the World.

Multi-colored Lights-- Luke 2:10; Psalm 2:8. The nations, tribes, and races of the earth; all who are invited into the Kingdom of God, can be seen in multi-colored lights on a tree.

The Star-- Matthew 2:21; Revelation 22: 16. The star of the east, guiding the Magi, and also Jesus, Himself, Who is the Bright and Morning Star.

Gifts-- John 3:16; 1 Corinthians 12; Ephesians 4:8, 11-13. Jesus, God's greatest gift, as well as, the Gifts of Jesus to the Church; the Holy Spirit, the Spirit's baptism, Spiritual gifts, and ministry gifts. (See Chapter 8)

Bells-- Zechariah 14:20; Isaiah 9:7. Bells are reminders of the Everlasting Kingdom of Christ.

Snowflakes-- Psalm 19:1. Each one is different, and they reveal the uniqueness of God's Creation.

Spheres/Globes/Balls-- Hebrew 12:1; 11:3. The earth, being round, under Christ Jesus' eternal Lordship can be seen in such ornaments.

Apples-- Matthew 1:21. As ornaments on the tree, an old French symbol of original sin, overcome (hung) by the Cross of the Lord Jesus Christ.

Toys, Models, Miniatures-- Psalm 24:1. Reminders, especially to children, of how all of play, life, and reality exists and really finds meaning in the Cross of Jesus.

The Candy Cane -- First mentioned in 1670 in Cologne, Germany, they were handed out to children during the long Christmas church services. They were bent at one end to imitate the shepherd's staff. First mention of red & white stripes was in 1900 in the U.S.

Father Christmas -- A figure associated with Christmas in numerous countries and cultures with Christian influence. Known by many names: Pere Noel, Padre Noel, Ded Moroz, Pai Natal, Babbo Natale, Kaghand Papik, Pare Noel, Mos Cracium, Noel Baba, and of course, Santa Claus. In Chronicles of Narnia, he is shown giving out gifts to the siblings, and declaring, "Merry Christmas, and Long Live Aslan!" Certainly one of the more controversial aspects of the holiday in some circles, but nevertheless a part of our culture of Christmas now is this figure. For me, I like to think of the fact, that at least, the "father" image and role is not lost in the holiday, even if somewhat and sometimes blurred. But the Scriptures reflect that the father role is important. Joseph was certainly a key figure in the birth of Christ. And somewhat yet mysterious as well. I just like the Scripture I offer here in this section of I Corinthians 4:15. "…you do not have many fathers….." So this year, you be that father as best you can, in the role you can supply to all. You won't regret it

Your Own Special Ornaments and Creative Arrangements – Robots, Star Wars, Star Trek ships, Legos, and special items that are specific to my family adorn our tree.

What are your special items and what do they mean to you and your family? List them below for future reference:

4 BIBLICAL EMBLEMS

Music and Song-- Luke 2: 13-14; Revelation 15:3-4. Christ's birth was heralded by angelic pronouncements and song. It is little wonder that one of the big things at Christmas time is music and specifically holiday music. One of the beauties of Christmas is the different expressions of music and genres during the holiday. Some of it is classic, and some tacky; but it is all good for keeping our thoughts on His first arrival.

The Crèche'-- Matthew 2:1-12; Luke 2:1-20. How do you teach people about Christ that can't read? St. Francis of Assisi had a solution: his creation of a live re-enactment of the Christmas story as a teaching aid to the illiterate people of the 13th Century in Europe. He was very wise to see the importance of symbols and that a story and a narrative could be communicated through "living stained glass" as it were. We still see them in our communities and it is one of the most recognizable activities associated with the holidays.

Animals-- Isaiah 11:6-10; Romans 8:18-23; Colossians 1:16. They are Christ's very own creations and a reminder that His redemption means ultimate removal of the curse that is on the earth.

Angels-- Matthew 1:20-25; 2:13-14; Luke 1:11-17, 26-38; 2:8-14. God's special messengers and an important part of Advent.

The Wise Men-- Matthew 2:1-12; Isaiah 60:3; Daniel 9:20-27. Likely a number of Persian scholars and astronomers seeking the fulfillment of Daniels prophecy about the Jewish Messiah.

The Shepherds-- Luke 2:8-20. The first to see and believe in Jesus.

5 CHILDREN AND CHRISTMAS

Luke 2:12; Mark 10:13-16. Jesus Christ was born as a child. This incarnation among other things, is God's eternal blessing upon children. The depth and consideration of the Incarnation is for common folk and theologians alike. But Christ did come as a baby; a child, and as you might expect, the Christmas holiday time is quickly associated among other thoughts, with children. Almost every great (and not so great) movie and film expressions of Christmas focus on children. Scrooge. The Grinch. Ralphie and the Red Rider BB gun. Even Captain Picard of Star Trek, in one of their movies, had a Christmas experience, which brings together the importance of Christ, our own "Christmas past" and futures, through the context of children.

For children, even though it seems that the Christmas push is all about being "in the moment" with them, the real long term impact for them, is the making of memories and validating and affirming them individually. Think about Christmas past for yourself. Sure you remember some of the gifts. But the core memories are rooted in the presence of people that love and care and extend that directly to the heart of the child. God came to us personally, and what we can do for a child at Christmas is to be there for them, personally. Not just the gift/stuff. It is about being there with them and connecting. Make it a priority that this year, you will be a positive presence for those children you love. Generations will thank you.

GOD BLESS US EVERY ONE

-Tiny Tim

6 EMMANUEL

"The virgin will conceive and give birth to a son, and they will call him Immanuel" (which means "God with us"). Matthew 1:23

Emmanuel, Emmanuel
His name is called Emmanuel
God with us
Revealed in us
His name is called Emmanuel
Bob McGee, 1976

Whether you use "Emmanuel" or "Immanuel" we are talking about the same person. And there is no doubt about the meaning. "God with us." Let that sink in. It is almost too much to absorb. Man has been trying to get to God in so many meaningless and empty ways. And God decided to take the situation into His own hands. He came Himself. He sent His Son.

Before there can be actions, there has to be a presence. Not only did Emmanuel come with the certainty that He would be "God with us," but then He added the additional claim of, "I will never leave you....." What a tremendous promise. Certainly there are quite a few topics that can be discussed and people of good will can and will differ on many subject. Yet there simply isn't any sophisticated way to interpret Matthew 28, "I will never leave you or forsake you." Many times, God first connects with us through people, situations, places, thoughts, and events. But the ultimate end is to be connected with Him.
It is my belief that it is this personal reality of Jesus Christ that moves and motivates us. Not just a concept, or a download, or a theological concept, but a personal reality of Christ. Presence; His presence.

Several years ago, I was at Emory Hospital in Atlanta, recovering from coronary bypass surgery. The circumstances of my recovery brought me to remaining in hospital on and through Christmas Eve. And the circumstances of life and the holiday had me alone in the hospital room for that night. It is a night I will never forget. The hospital staff was great. I was scheduled for discharge on the next day; Christmas Day, so my wife returned to the hotel to prepare for our return home. Since it was the holiday, the hotel staff had excused the hotel shuttle staff so they could be off and with family. My son had returned to Alabama to go back to work, and my local friends were also with family for the evening. So it was just me, alone, in the room on Christmas Eve. As I looked out my window north on Peachtree Street, I could see the literal twinkle of Christmas lights up the avenue. Several churches in view were having Christmas Eve services. I now know how that kid felt, sitting in the window of the hospital in the Home Alone movie. It was a really mixed batch of feelings. It is in these moments that we find out the reality, depth, and true value of how much we value the presence of Emmanuel.

The holidays can be a tough time for folks who are feeling disconnected for some reason or the other. But I can give a personal accounting of the fact, that because of Emmanuel, I will never, ever be alone again.

A Holiday Exercise:

If you are feeling a bit disconnected, I have a challenge for you. What is the numerical date of your birthday? Mine is the 20th. You want to make a difference for someone and be a link to Emmanuel? Are you willing to take a risk? Then during the holidays, pick out a small Christmas ornament of yours, or go buy one. Then go to the nearest nursing home or long term care facility near you. Walk in, and go to the corresponding room of your birth date. Take the ornament and let things happen. They will be changed and so will you.

7 ADVENT WREATH

"Advent":

1) The arrival of a notable person, thing, or event.

2) The season leading up to Christmas and including the four preceding Sundays

3) The second coming of Christ

Advent is a cosmic "macro" event that touches and impacts the individual. The coming of Christ slices history and marks time in a remarkable way.

The Advent Wreath is a small, but very powerful way to weave the concepts of the first coming of Christ with His promised second

We can thank our 16th century German Lutheran brethren for the Advent wreath as it is generally presented these days. (Colbert, 1996). In a sort of St. Francis of Assisi move, a Lutheran minister in the 19th century, working with poor children who were constantly bugging him about when Christmas would come, decided to use their curiosity to teach the Word. (Sound familiar?) So he took an old wagon cart wheel, and put candles on it. In his version there was a candle lit every day, and on Sunday a big white candle was lit. Over time it was shrunk down to a smaller wreath with four candles for each Sunday and a fifth on Christmas Day. Through the early part of the 20th century the custom spread through Roman Catholic and Protestant churches and eventually found its way to the U.S. before World War II.

Beyond that, there are a lot of variations, colors of candles, and sequence of attached meaning and remembrance for each of the four candles lit on successive Sunday's before Christmas Day. Violet, rose, and blue are some of the colors. Whatever works for you, do it. The general sequence of significance and theme for the candles is week one, hope; week two, peace; week three, joy; and week four, love. And of course, on Christmas Day is the Christ Candle or at our house, the Jesus Birthday Candle. Our tradition at our house of candle sequence is this, with some collateral thoughts and meditations:

Week One- The Prophecy Candle.
Consider how Christmas is Disruptive
Isaiah 9:6-7

Week Two- The Bethlehem Candle.
Consider miracles: little and big ones
Matthew 2:1ff

Week Three- The Shepherds Candle.
Shepherds: Mundane and Amazing
Luke 2:8ff

Week Four- The Angels Candle.
Luke 2:13-15

Christmas Day – The Jesus Candle

Of course there are many other
Scriptures that go with each topic of the
week. I leave it for you to read and find
them for yourself.

8 GOD'S GIFT

There are at least six words in the New Testament that are translated into the one English word, "gift." Five of the most significant of them are shared in this chapter.

So it is at Christmas, that gifts are a central part of the event, for better or worse. Rather than ignore or try to deflect, I say, let's dig down and gain a better understanding of the idea of gift. The best way to do so, is to take a look at each word from the original Greek of the ancient Bible texts, and consider each one.

Doron – "to give" This word describes the act or action of giving a present for celebration of an occasion. Whether to help people, or to God as an offering, or whatever, it is the action of giving and letting go of something to someone else. Clearly, this word makes a connection of our holiday activity. It is Biblical to give to people gifts.

Dorea – "a free gift of God of a spiritual or supernatural nature." 2 Corinthians 9:15 is the best example of the use of this word.

Whatever we give as a gift during the holidays, it is rooted in the "indescribable gift" of God to us: His Son Jesus Christ.

Doma – "a gift that reflects the character of the giver, more than the value of the gift." Matthew 7:11 Remember "A Christmas Carol"? When Scrooge emerged on Christmas morning as a changed man, he started giving almost immediately. And the quality of his gifts reflected his transformation. They weren't necessarily expensive; they were directed in a practical and personal way. (I am partial to the 1938 version.)
Dosis – "the act of giving as a topic or source subject" James 1:17 Again, there is no way to differentiate the holidays from giving. It is a big topic.

Charisma – "a gift wrapped and saturated with grace or graciousness," but not just a thing or item. The undeserved gift is soaked and brimming with the ability to have an impact beyond what anyone might imagine. I received such a gift the week of Christmas, 2015, as I had heart surgery and went home on Christmas Day with the gift of physical life. I can say that God has blessed me with spiritual gifts as well, that have allowed me to serve Him and see "an impact beyond what anyone might imagine." That's just God.

As we reflect on the birth of Christ, his first Advent was simply the beginning in so many ways. And let us never forget this incredible reality:

Romans 6:23 For the wages of sin [is] death; but the gift of God [is] eternal life through Jesus Christ our Lord.

9-THE SECOND ADVENT

Christmas time is a promise. It is an awakening, twinkling lights, song, music, fresh baked goods, candles, beautifully and carefully wrapped packages, parties, celebrations, worship services. But there is something else in the air. Do you feel it? It's the coming Kingdom. It is the return of Christ. No more tears, nor crying or mourning. There is a sound and a message embedded in our Christmas time. Just as surely as Jesus came the first time, he himself has said he will return.

"Yes, I am coming soon." Amen. Come, Lord Jesus. Revelation 22:20

Wouldn't it be great if he came Christmas Day?

10- TWO NEAT FUN ACTIVITIES

I. Christmas Tree on the Cover—

You will need various color construction paper, glue sticks, and then the background paper that you plan to put it on. The background paper can be any neutral cover. Then, take scissors or a paper cutter, and cut out long strips of colored paper of the various colors and lengths: especially different shades of green, and put those aside. Then you cut out all different colors of the other construction paper, in various lengths and colors. Turn your background page, vertical. Then starting at the top of your background paper, you start gluing down various shades of green strips. At the top, put the shorter pieces of paper, diagonally and overlapping. As you go down the page, make the strips longer, continuing in the diagonal direction. Make sure you have different shades of green colors throughout the tree that are overlapping. You don't have to worry about the trunk. Then go back, and repeat the same procedure with your multi-colored construction strips of paper that you have previously cut. Short strips go at the top, and as you go down the tree, keep gluing them down diagonally with increasing lengths. Finish with a brown trunk square at the bottom if you want, and a star or other emblem at the top.

II. The Candy Cane Project

Cut out the stencil or make a copy from the one provided here in the book. Place stencil on sturdy paper, and trace around the stencil with a pencil, and draw in the strips as you want them on the Candy Cane. Don't use a ruler, but draw them by hand. The lines should curve slightly. (See picture). Do not over do the stripes, approximately 6 to 10 stripes should be sufficient. Color the stripes whatever you prefer, using crayons, colored pencils, or whatever your choice. Traditional is red and white, but also green and white, and green, red, and white are used too. Then cut out the Candy Cane. I would use a glue stick and glue it down to your choice of a piece of construction paper. Embellish the background or the Candy Cane as desired. Suggestions: if using black construction paper as background, you can draw stars, and use glitter on the stars. Or put a bow on the Candy Cane as well. Have fun.

The Candy Cane Stencil (to copy)

A finished example of the Candy Cane
Project…...

11- PHOTO STORIES

The choice of the photos in the book are very intentional.

Christmas Tree Farm photo from Shells Tree Farm near Tuscumbia, AL (ii)

Leyland Cyprus Tree in Dining Room, our 12 foot tree, in 2008. (p. 4)

Christmas Cat Decorations and Welcome Station on our porch, as we reach out to "every creature." (p. 12)

Whoville on Christmas morning. Their worship was not dependent on the "stuff" the Grinch could take; their focus was on a Greater One. (p. 14)

Shepherd's Ornament. Love it. (p. 22)

Celtic Style Advent Wreath. Creative. (p. 27)

Bubble Light. Big symbol of Christmas to me. (p. 30)

Crèche Ornament from our decorations. (p. 32)

The Charlie Brown Christmas Tree. I could write a book just on this part of my life. Residents of Russellville, AL were familiar with it. It is a cedar tree that grew up through cracks in a wall in our yard. I reminded me of the one from the Charlie Brown Christmas. I put a string of lights on it, and anytime it snowed, I turned it on. My rationale was, "it is Christmas somewhere." The picture was taken on Armenian Christmas Day in January of the year. (P. 34)

ABOUT THE AUTHOR

Alan Bragwell is also the author of the book, "Reality: Dreams and Hard Facts." He has been a licensed professional counselor in Alabama since 1998, and is a graduate of Regent University. He is sought and serves as a consultant and advisor to medical practices, ministries, churches, and various organizations on a national and international level. His past ministry experience coupled with his clinical expertise makes him a useful resource in complicated situations. He is married to Debra Williams Bragwell and they live in Florence, AL.